A FOR THIS LOVE OF MINE

RHONDA CLARKE
VOLUME

1

ACKNOWLEDGEMENT

Let me thank all those who have hurt me, curse me, and abuse me, you inspired me, thanks to my English teacher, Mr. Eusi Kwayana who thought me how to write poems, thanks to Ms. Sukhdeo who has played a role in my life by being my English teacher in L'Amoreaux C.I, you always give me hope and was always willing to spend that extra time with me in school to make me be a better person in writing, A special thanks to my children, Robert, Randy and Robin for causing me to understand and appreciate love, thanks to my mother Lorna Williams for showing me love which has enable love in me, thanks to my sister and my nephew H. Dwayne Williams for motivating me to publish my book because they belief I had great talent and they wouldn't want to see me waste it, thanks to pastor Jeune St. Clair for always asking me to write a poem every time for events in church, though I was shy, my children proudly and bravely read my poems and made me very proud. Thanks to my friends who would always ask me to write something for their boyfriend or girlfriend for them to pretend it was written by them, you give me courage, thanks to my fiancé for telling me," babe you should publish your book, I don't know what you're waiting for. Thanks to my aunt Sandra who told me I should just get a compilation of all my poems and publish one big book, you bless me, my nieces and my nephews, my cousins, and my Facebook friends, thank you for always liking, sharing, commenting on my poems, whatever you've said to me, be it good or bad, it has caused me great improvement or caused me to appreciate the poem presented to you, don't stop sharing and loving and commenting, my nephew Shane McDonald, thank you for asking me to write a piece for your deceased grandmother, you received a standing ovation and that has caused me to be more known for what I do and to tell you the truth, others came by asking me to write for them and their love ones, thanks to my children school, Chester Le senior public school who has heard of me and after looking at some of my poems, have published one in their weekly news pamphlet, thanks to those who didn't know I was a poet but upon reading my poems in the school pamphlet, flooded my door and cried because my poems have touched them in one way or the other. Thanks to my exes who lied and cheater, you inspired me, in al of my poems, someone or something inspired me and Im thankful for all contribution, be it negative or positive, I want you to know that I heard you and felt for you, I hope all my readers will be touched in one way or another by reading one or more of my poems, I look forward in your feedback if any through my social platforms. Thank you.

TABLE OF CONTENTS

GIVE ME A HEART	9
DONT	11
TELL ME	12
ONE NIGHT	13
ALIVE	14
RETURN	15
YOU	16
WEATHER	17
MY FINAL	18
GIVE ME	19
MY ROCK	20
WRONG	21
SON	23
MY SON	25
A MOTHER'S LOVE	26
MY LOVE	29
ONE DAY	31
ALLOW ME	32

MY MOM	33
WAITED FOR US	34
YOU MOTHER	39
YOU	41
MY EVERYTHING	42
I LONG	44
NONE LIKE HER	45
THANK YOU MOTHER	47
A MOTHERS LOVE	49
ABSENCE	51
WITHOUT WARNING	52
IN LOVE WITH YOU	53
WERE YOU THERE	54
YOU'VE TAKEN ME	56
MOMENTS	57
EYES	58
CURRENTLY	59
LOVE	60
TEMPERATURE	61

A FRIEND	62
HOMELESS	63
IT IS YOUR LOVE	64
YOU AND ME	66
AUTHENTICATED LOVE	67
MOTHER	71
MY EVERYTHING	74
THANK YOU	76
PROTECTING YOU	78
MISS YOU	79
OVERCAME	80
LAY YOU DOWN	82
ITS YOU	83
YOU AND YOUR LOVE	84
DISTANCE	85
THE ONE	86
RETURN	87
DON'T	88
MY ONLY LOVE	89

YOU	90
ME	92
WAIT	93
JUDGE NOT MY LOOKS	94
HE	95
About the Author	97

GIVE ME A HEART

Give me a heart that's never been broken
Give me a heart that won't be forsaken
Give me a heart that will be spoken
Give me a heart that doesn't need to be hemmed
Give me a heart that knows no stain
Give me a heart that protects its heart from pain
Give me a heart that seeks in me for joy
Give me a heart that will play with me like a toy
Give me a heart that seeks to ploy
Give me a heart that knows what to treasure
Give me a heart that knows how to pleasure
Give me a heart that knows how to measure
Give me a heart that joins me in bed
Give me a heart that lays beside me head to head
Give me a heart that brightens up my day
Give me a heart that will not cause me to worry
Give me a heart who will make my gloomy days okay
Give me a heart that will never cause me dismay
Give me a heart that will forever stay
Give me a heart that will grow old and grey with me
Give me a heart that will love me after I'm dead and face decay
Give me a heart whose love will never go away

For a heart as such, I so long, for a heart as such will never do me wrong
For a heart as such I pray, though it's challenging to find such heart today

DONT

Don't take me out of the light, only to leave me in the dark
Don't love me to part, don't love me to break my heart
Don't take me away from what I like, to leave me in fright
Don't take me it won't be right, if you'll want me just for a few nights
Don't take me to the top to drop me at the bottom, why they do that? I never fathom
Don't bring me to the top; I'm afraid of height
Don't take away my day for lonely nights
Don't take me heavy to drop me light
Don't take me; I'd rather stay here tonight
Don't take me if it's not for life
Don't take me if I won't be your wife

TELL ME

You're so sexy
You're so sweet
Your lips are so juicy, and you're so sweet
Tell me of the things you eat
After making love, I fall asleep
Don't think I'm weak
Just every time I see you, my heart skips a beat
I get nervous by your smiles
That look from your eyes
I know this love will survive.

ONE NIGHT

One night, Exploring, the path leads to gold
One night, all kinds of stories our bodies told
One night, I thought, this one, I'll hold
One night, follow me down the path
One night, if you want my heart
One night, here on forth, let's make the start

ALIVE

Though we've led separate lives
If love still lives come into my hive
Cause I want to keep this love alive

RETURN

Ignite and resonate the sparks once known between us

For no matter where I be strayed,

You're that wind to my dust

YOU

You're the most profound depth of my heart
I pray we would never part
So let's continue what we start
No one in this world pleases me like you do
Yes I've strayed, but love has brought me back to you

WEATHER

Hold my hand if you desire to dream together
If you can love me in various weather
Oceans roughest tide, are you willing to ride?
There is no coping without you, no life.
Until you take me as your wife

MY FINAL

My first, my final, you are my one
With you my life must end for with you it began
Just the very whisper of you undress me
Without you, my existence would be an empty vessel
Landing In places, I do not wish to be
And I will never put our love in jeopardy
For you are the one for me

GIVE ME

Without you, my life will be that of a thistle
Could you give me your hand smooth, not bristle?
And to me, you'll be entitled
I'll be yours, forever gentle
From searching I'm outwrestled
Together, let's dwell in your castle
For we've survived the battle
Cling to me and let's blow the whistle

MY ROCK

My twinkling rock, my dreams come through
I'm blessed to shared moments with you
Deposited love, never to flee, I'm stuck with thee
Exploration has caused me to thirst your love
When I thought that we were through,
Beaten up, I am, by my needs of you,
Love has brought me back where I belong
I'm consumed by a strong love
My appetite prevails in wanting you
In my wander and stray, I'm susceptible to your glue.

WRONG

I've done you wrong, and so, afar, I stayed
I've done you wrong, to have you back I prayed
For I've loved you amidst, time apart
I've done you wrong, my teacher, and ruler of my heart
Where ever I go, there you park
Time away from you led me to discover
You're the light in my darkest hour
Like an archaeologist, I probe to find
That which was already mine
I thirst for someone who was never lost
Forgive me, a fool, for I was blind
Grip my hand; let's find stairs to our Love
My good night sleep and my awaken morning
Tell me I'm your only darling
To your every wish I intend to comply
For your Love, I can't defy, for on your Love I rely
Tickle my palm and tell me I'm your hearts core
Tell me you loved me, and desire to love me more
Time away from you made me lonely and crossed
Time away from you made me blue
Time away from you showed me I love you true

Sad and lost, I couldn't stop thinking of you
I strayed and endured the cost,
Your Love saturates and quenches my thirst
Your Love brought me, back to my nurse

SON

My son, though you are eighteen, I'll never let you go
You'll always be my love; I hope your love will continue to flow
From conception and forever, you're my son, and I'll never leave you alone
When you're out, I'll still wait up until you come home
Your earnings might be little and slow, but we both know where fast cash can lead tomorrow
It leads only to pain, regrets and sorrow
Join not your friends in crime, for if you do, you'll befit the time
I'm begging you, stay far from that lime, and don't be a number on a file
Continue to earn your living tile by tile, and you'll always see me smile
I've given you my love every time, ensuring your days was still fine
I've ever shown love to you my son
Figured ways to make your days fun
Always holding hands and remedying your sickness and cold
Though time has passed and you're all grown, the memories of you I'll dearly hold

It is the same kind of love that has seen you through
the same kind of love, its old but yet new, love I'll always have for you
Yes I'm proud, I'm happy, I'm giving thanks to God for seeing you through
For as your mother I want you to smile continuously
For no matter what, you are my child
And ill guide you always and not for a while

MY SON

Even if through death I should leave this placed
My love for you will never be erased
These words I'm saying must never go to waste
Consider it golden and tell it to your friend
For this love I've got for you will never know an end
I swear, my love will never disappear
It's me your mother, the one who will always care
I love without benefit or gain
Yet I aim to prevent you from pain
I want your investment to bring you profit
You've got worth from your birth so let not anyone
treat you like dirt
For if you're in pain, I'll only hurt
Come over here, let me tell you something
Let me remind you of the joy you bring
It's because of you, I sing
I love you and wish you'd never forget your blessing

A MOTHER'S LOVE

She thinks in her head; she earns bread without the inclusion of the fed

I subscribe to precise motherly Love, she takes a risk without any fears

Motherly stress with no aide, my school fees, she paid

Though depressed was her heart, and rugged her path

She fights to brighten her cloth and to save them from the wrath

She stays focused on her mission

Her seeds are important and immediate, her pride possession

Though hungry, her starving stomach she'll ignore

To feed her children, and even give them more

Though late, she'll provide a plate

For the Love of her kids, she ignores a date

If faced with problems, she'll run to my aide

When I'm asleep, she opens the door and takes a peep

She'll grab her bible and kneeled, there she weep

Praying I'll never go to the slam

She eats less while my plate, she rams

With tears flushing down her eyes, she cries, father let my children rise

Though every area of her life, the devil seems to compromise

She fights like she's got no other choice

No one knows her history yet they criticize

But I'm proud of you mother your life is not in disguise

For all the trouble I've given you I wish I could wipe away your pain

I love you mama, and I will never cause you disgrace and shame

Your mere existence is what I love; I put the crown to your name

You're the Love that entwines in my honey, I love you mommy

MY LOVE

I'll always love you sure

I love you from my heart's core

They displayed jealousy, because I'm spending time with my mommy

My life is bright because you shape me right

A decent young lady with a law degree

You are the reason I can be

Cooked, cleaned and fed me lots, I cried hungry; you started the pot

My meal was always hot

You fed me; you did not forget

To you, I take off my hat; I love you mother, you're all I got

To me you're like a god, though you never speared me the rod

A good mother, you never endanger me,
though life was hard

Somehow, you've been dealt the wrong card

But for your struggle, here is your reward

Anything you want, as long as I live

My last penny, to you I'll give

For you love me and never grow weary

As long as I live, I don't want you to worry

And so of your needs, let me worry

ONE DAY

You're the glitter in the sky that only my eye sees

You're that cool breeze in the midst of February

The greenest of grass existing upon earth

One day mother I'll show you what you're worth

ALLOW ME

Allow me, a child
To immerse myself
Doing the things, I love and desire to do
Rather than the things my parents love and desire for me to do
I want to live my life fulfilling my dreams and not that of my parents

MY MOM

How could man tell me not to talk to my mom?
To hate and never care for mom
To tell lies and spread false rumours of mom
Taint you and create a destructive path for mom
Wishing life worst wrath for mom
No man can never love me like my mom
If I'm sick, I can call my mom
I love her, and that's my mom.
If man understood, this wouldn't be a thought.
A man like you is a man without a heart.
You don't know what mothers are worth.
Mother was there from the start.
You can't make me and my mother part.
My mother over man
Many are they reside on this land.
I've got one mother in this nation.
I refuse to fulfill man's demand.
When I'm a little girl, my mother held my hand.
So if you don't like her, pick up your things and gwan
My mother give me life.
My mother provided the rice.
I love you, but seek elsewhere for your wife.
Because I could never be cold to my mother like ice

WAITED FOR US

Though your love had gone astray, and during such moment, my heart most considerable dismay

Confiscated was your love daily. Our encounter is no accident; hence my reason for never going astray.

Embedded in my heart is undying love for you.

I pondered not that this is evidently true love, for true love does not eternally abandon its heart's bottom

So rather than mourn your love, I've fasted for your love.

Even as my heart hurts, I somehow persevered in love rather than collapse in love.

In an imperfect world, we lacked abilities to adhere to affectionate love though forever I'll hold on.

Challenges want to take hold, but escorted are my thoughts and beliefs to your heart.

And tailored is my heart to love you eternally.

Even as I faced the void, embraced was moments vividly memorable.

Two people with preferences and differences, be you, spare from wrath.

In this imperfect world, our lights cannot be eternally dimmed, for our love has been preordained.

Amidst your absence, my heart grew to love you instead of retire from loving you.

Even in trying times of seemingly, crumbling, and failing love, I thirst for your love and your touch.

There within, lingers, harbored, and compiled love for you, though you haven't had a clue.

Though all that you have done, none can substantiate my departure from your love

I merely angered no more, for comprehension of the term love, appears boldly, even as we were apart.

I've refrained from worries, instead, surrounded my thoughts with encouragement, thee forget how to fret.

During your absence, my heart has faced many interrogations, yet I've navigated and escalated in our love.

Afflicted, yet I've surrendered to you in love and escalated in stubbornness toward failure engaging my heart and mind with thoughts of you through challenges and sacrifices and an affiliation of compassionate and a non-conflicting mind.

Comb my heart, and you'll find nothing but vast possession of my love disseminating for you.

A love compacted with the substance of perseverance and armed with a heart escalating in unquestioning love.

The source of my love drive, here we are together, and all feels justified.

A Devine strategy has allowed our love survival.

Our hearts collided in the vicinity of eternity, an appointed meeting of precision.

A love once delayed but never denied, here we are, a work in progress.

Unpleasant acts are suffocated, dimmed was the light of perfection, but the imperfect has now been perfected.

We've face challenges with the aim of embarking upon our destiny.

Accurate was the vicinity of our meeting, with the substance of perseverance, my heart has bypassed injury.

For we are curators armed with ingredients to cure our love

Innocently, we've faced trials, but perseverance prevailed causing our great love endurances

Uninterrupted focus and discipline has brought me to you; two minds navigating in one destination.

My love for you is not a dramatization but authenticated through faith.

With Uninterrupted focus and admiration, I've stayed true to you.

Despite interrogations, escalated is my love for you.

Nothing that you may do can substantiate my departure from our love.

My mind radiates nothing but love for you, affliction fails, and love forever reigns.

My heart forever perpetuates love for you.

All these years of confessing, my confessions are true, for my love is undoubtedly for you.

I love you this much hence the reason I did not quit.

Though Afflictions may poke, with adjoining hands, in love we're forever soak

A love appointed by our father is a love we will eternally treasure

Our hearts' are coming from where love hails, so all interruptions are bound to fail.

For in love we will prevail

YOU MOTHER

Launched and conducted you have architecture my life, Defended and corrected my wrongs
Though I've imposed extreme difficulties upon your life, yet you love me though I should have been defied
Even Though I've constipated, constrained and caused you great pain
You still love me through all my faults; you've not complained
From loving you, I can never refrain
Because you've solely affiliated yourself with my upbringing and my survival
For all your Heartache and pain, my love you've forever gained
For as long as I have breath, anything you want, you will get, and my love for you will only reign
You've translated my sickness to great health and happiness
You're the force of my life, my drive, the reason I thrive
For you've captured my pain and threw it down the drain
The detector of my problems and an instigator of my joy
Your love is the reason why I've changed my ways

Due to Corrected path and kept loved in your heart
Despite complications, you still love me
A vision of my happiness
Your promotion of love your love for me makes me feel unconquered and superior
You'll always be loved, for you first love me
You've thought me how to be happy and free
Your love unveils my love; you're the perfection in me, you've curtailed
Without your labor, sacrifice, willingness, strength and love
Your guidance and securities for the central outlook of me
Your love has no length; it's more than a plaster to my strength
Your love can never be replaced for your love is my savings grace
All things I do is affiliating with you
The source of my love
My love, you are very much glued and cemented
A love that will never be fermented
For in my upbringing, you did not fail
And when I felt down, you were always there
I love you, mother, because you truly care
And I thank you for indulging in my troubling affairs

YOU

My love, you've tamed
For my heart, you've gained the fame
Love forever gain, from your love; I cannot refrain
Yes I forever love you, and you'll never hear me complain
Your love satisfies me again and again
From you, honey bee, I can never grow weary
I can't think of an end
For you feel like heaven, send

MY EVERYTHING

My little bee, I knew you were the one for me

You've come into my life and showed me all that I can be

You've opened up doors for me to fulfill my fantasies

You've taken me to a place call ecstasy

Loving you enables me to be loving, caring and free

Having you in my life had to be destiny

My morning coffee and my midnight tea

What the future holds is yet to be told

But with you, I found a diamond, yes I've surpassed gold

With you in my life, no price can't be summarize

I really love how you entice

Daily I embark upon beautiful surprises

This is real love, no catch or disguises

The supplier of love to my body, love to my life

Now everyone wants to learn from our enterprise

Whenever I opened my mouth, it's of you that I speak

Baby boy, our love is on fleet

This love of ours is established on solid ground

No scale can't weigh it, not by pint or pound

Indeed our love surpass all royalty

A love they will never know until they eat fruit from our tree

This our love is truly divine

I proudly say to the world; you're mine

No other love is like our love

We worry not for our love is shielded by wings of dove

No other love could be like this

For you've swept me off my feet with one kiss

With aroma of sweet pitch pine

From all other activities, I've resigned

For your love is nothing but the plus sign

For your love, I was designed

And you and I will forever love in drought and famine

For all of life's love, you are my lifeline

And loving you lights up my heart brighter than the world sunshine

I LONG

How I long to be this brave
To look you into your eyes and say words like these
To tell you this love I have for you can never be denied
For all your hurt and sufferings, I deeply cried
A brave face, I've put on
But inside, I'm not as strong
Oh, mother, days of weeping and tears are over
How I salute to you in high and low places
Though the trials and tribulations of my upbringing was not easy
You've never ceased from striving; your love was still outpouring
And for this belief you are the pedals to my proceeding
The light to my sight
The pencil to my paper
I'm proud you are my mother.

NONE LIKE HER

You evoke my joy and Fadeaway my sorrow
Because of you, I'm not worried about tomorrow
What a good seed you've sowed
Let me reap for I've planted and watched you grow
Evolve into something great, and I want the world to know
Tears of joy, from my eyes, it flows
Woman, you weren't meant to struggle for long
Raising kids alone, yes the father is long gone
Held it up, mama, you're so strong
A good seed, I fell right into your plan
Looking back, the struggle, mama, I understand
Many nights no food in the pot, the struggle was really hot
But through your perseverance, we've made it, and of the struggle, I won't forget
I can't forget how you came close to quitting though you choose not, it was a fight
And your determination caused you to deserve it all tonight
For the decisions you've made hard and right
When we asked you to buy bread, you looked at us and held your head in fear

Tears down your precious face, your greatest despair
What a lifestyle dread
You've not placed me in a position of abandonment
You've spent on me, your every cent; now I will forever pay your rent
They know not our storm, nothing about your numerous exposure to germs
Mother, you're a very precious one, worth more than diamonds and pearl
A positive instigator, you're my world
A creator and mind shaper
A director, constantly sharing and caring
Genuine and empathetic
You let your child have her last
You ignores our negative past
You're always there in times of sorrow
You'll love me years after tomorrow

THANK YOU MOTHER

Oh mother, so many things I wish to say
Tears of joy as I look your way
I don't know how to start, so I'll just say, "thank you."
No devil can put me down and under
Because I got you, your love is much stronger
Every time I wink, Of you I think
Let me tell you something
You'll never understand what joy you bring
When I'm down and feel like crying
I simply think of you, and I start smiling
The one who cooks and clean for me
I'm so glad you are my mommy
Thank you for teaching me that I will and I can
Your teaching has caused me to be a better man
All the many things I could not do on my own
You've rescued me when I was a trap
It is things like this I can never forget
You've fetched me away from life misery
And placed me in a place where I'm now free
It's because of you I can now be
And so I'd like to say "thank you, mommy."
My days of pain is over

Thank you for shielding me from danger and lending me your shoulders
Thank you for accompanying me through my darkest nights
And encouraging me to believe everything will be alright
Though the danger was real
Mother, you made me feel
Just like my darkest times so must you be in my brightest days
Oh mother I just intend to show you some ways
Embedded in my heart is love for you

A MOTHERS LOVE

A mother's love is all I know for my daddy packed up and let her go

Painful was the task for me to grow

But with mammas love every good thing flow

When daddy run away, you've worked night and day

To put food on the table and those bills you've paid

Encouraged us to bring home good grades

We come home daily to the hot food you've made

I'm who I am because of your love, your aide

I will love you always, because of you I am made

You've raised us on your own

Reap the benefit of the seed you've sown

There could never be a mother like you even if you're a clown

Mamma your love is so empowering

Only you put up with everything.

You fought for us though vast is the troubles we bring

In times of trouble, the only mamma gives in.

They will never understand the love she has within.

But through every stare, I see your despair, your modern warfare.

Your heart in places it should not be all caused by the troubles of me.

But I will set your weary heart free, Free from the burden and free from stress.

Free from unwanted situations clustering your nest

I love you, mother, for you are the best.

ABSENCE

Let me catch those tears of guilt
Let it soak up my kilt
Your presence was a mist
Then into the woods, you were amidst
No trace of your scent
I didn't know where you went
But your absence escorted me and encouraged me to prevail
In the arms of another, I swiftly sail
And he's been loving me just when you fail.

WITHOUT WARNING

Without warning, the pipe shuts off
Without notice, no water in the hose
And he made me take off my clothes
Yes I took off my blouse
I had prepared for a night of noise
But suddenly the pipe close
Without warning, I'm left confused
He told me he'd leave me to bruise
But without warning, he loose
This day I choose
I blended and juiced, I prepared for this swing
Without warning, sex becomes a sin
Without warning, he begins to grin
I always lose, and he always wins
One to two minutes and he's clocked in
What a thing
I waited for him to water my grass
I waited for him to grip my ass
But without warning, he was the weaken ass
Who give little performance yet eat grass

IN LOVE WITH YOU

It's true; I am in love, the day I met you
My love pierce through the brightest sky for you
In all that I do, I think about you
The clock struck the hour, and I'm thinking about you
I'm wearing specific attire, and I'm thinking about you
My desire, my heart requires, I always think of you
Never know I would express love this way for you
I love you with deep meaning
My love reaches the ceiling
You're my darling
I'm feeling something great for you
Feelings I can't let go
I've got to let you know, let it flow
I love you today and will love you tomorrow
If you believe in us, let's reap what we sow
From low cut to afro
That's the love I've got for you

WERE YOU THERE

Were you there when I leaped into pain?
Were you there when I cried tears like rain?
Were you there to answer my call or to carry me through the dark?
Were you there to make me laugh in the park?
Were you there when I was scared of the dark?
Were you there to pick me up from a fall?
Were you there to tell me things was alright
Were you there to tuck me in good night?
Were you there to discourage me from fights?
Were you there to teach me wrong from right?
Were you there in my sight?
Were you there when my heartfelt bitter?
Were you there when I was a hill?
Were you there to give me a pill?
Were you there when I struggle with life?
Were you there to discourage me from strife?
Were you there when I pick up the knife?
Were you there when I was about to take a life
Were you there when I was sick and cold?
Were you there when I score my first goal?
Were you there when my tears poured?
With a brave face, you were gone

I applaud my mother for being strong
Were you there from my begging?
Were you there to protect me from sin?
Were you there when I was close to perish, a star, my presence you don't wish to miss
Were you there, what moments of us, do you cherish?
The one where you wished I was aborted, perish
Now you hug and kiss.
But I say, for your presence, I do not wish
For you were not there, and I've nothing to reminisce.

YOU'VE TAKEN ME

You've taken me to a place I will always cherish
You've taken me to a place of whip cream with peach
You've taken me to that place, teach baby teach
You've taken me to a place under your sheet
You've taken me to a place where I'll always sleep
You've taken me to a place where I have love to keep
You've taken me to a place where I'm complete

MOMENTS

Wine and roses
Sexy poses
A time to entwine, thank you for being mine
Celebrating, for we shine
Fondue, strawberries and chocolates are no crime
It's just the way I like to spend your time
Kiss me, whip me, and be not sorry; I'll be fine
Sweet conversation over red wine
Keep me here, solitary confine.

EYES

I knew you love me your eyes told me so
They grip me tight and refuse to let me go
You walked away, but of me, you needed more
My clothes you've ripped and tore
So many kisses, nipples, they're soar
You wished to make me your Misses
Clean me up like dishes
You swing me left; you swing me right
Slowly, I'm going out of sight
And on my body, you wrestled, a fight
Though this isn't real
The eyes cause you to feel
Try catching me in the afterlife
For this was just another dreamy night
And you won't be loving me tonight

CURRENTLY

Let me hold your hand while you carry my clutch
If only you could feel the tingling of my crutch
Loving you has cause such
It happens every time we touch
Fingers running through my hair
Jumping, no panties, I didn't wear
Eyes as brown as yours
I just want to drop the purse
Take it away; you might hear my outburst
Your loving I thirst
Can you be my last, though not my first?

LOVE

Your love wraps me up like a snake
When I'm asleep, I don't want to wake
You give me love; my body can take
I love you, real love, not fake
I'll be your Rihanna; you be my drake
For your loving, I'm always ready to participate
Ejaculation feels like an earthquake
Don't stop baby, dominate
Give me good loving, don't terminate
I will always want your loving in the immediate
Hit me right there, baby penetrate
Good loving, to your love I gravitate

TEMPERATURE

Cold to the touch
Love don't have to be as such
But a warm hand can pull my stands
When I check my blueprint, you've got the hand.

A FRIEND

I'm looking for roots in my life, not branches or leaves
Not the ones who will lie to me and cause me grief
Not the one who will deny me and leave
Not the ones, of my love, they are thieves
But the one who will hug me with a tight squeeze
Not the one who will judge me and cause me to be displeased
But the one who will assure me of a beautiful end and cause me to be pleased
That's who I call a friend
You don't need strife to see my end
You have an understanding and can comprehend

HOMELESS

Homeless and broke, embrace it
Change will come, you'll make it
The ground may be your bed, and the bugs may crawl over your head
The branches might be your shed, but one day you will no longer beg
You'll have space so long and wide; you can spread your leg
Homelessness will be a thing of your past, for you will know greener grass
You won't be sleeping in people's tent, but people will be paying you rent
Then you'll wonder, where homelessness went

IT IS YOUR LOVE

I love you now as I did then
If I'm to love again, I'll choose to love you till the end
I felt it, and of it, I'm sure, I'll love you until I can't love anymore
Love can be stifled but never killed; I knew you'd be mine for its God's will
It is love when I can't go without hearing your voice
It is love when love has left me without a choice
It is love when on your chest I easily fall asleep
It is love that makes me love you and love to keep
It is love, forever since you've come into my life I no longer weep
It is love that has caused me to love you this deep
Your love has caused me to dream again
Your love brings me joy and eradicate pain
It is your love that makes me feel satisfied
It is your love; I want to hold onto, until I die
It is because of your love, and I can love you without a try
It is your love that enables me to lift my head up high
When the sun goes down, and you're not around, I would feel lost until you have been found

When you're not near, I'm susceptible to fear
With you around, turn off the light, I don't care, for the one I love is right here
It is your love. I'd be damn to deny
Your love is the reason I no longer cry

YOU AND ME

Love is an eternal reign.
With you in my life, we've got the world to gain
Your love is a symbol of my strength, courage, and perseverance
Your love resonates in me, for your love is the reason I can be
Thank you for allowing your love to set me free
My love has been arrested and detained with a unique key
A key buried into your heart, where only my love visits
No other love can access this key, for it is only accessible to you and me!
My love is enveloped and entwined in the depths of your heart, and so be it, we are inseparable for wherever you go there is my love also.
We are the topic of our togetherness; your love strengthens my heart.
We're trapped in a never-ending convo and an everlasting stride, shall we enjoy the ride?
You're all I adore; I'll always be needing your love more and more.
None can kill what's god's will.
You're the essence of my life.
And I can't wait to be your wife.

AUTHENTICATED LOVE

Confiscated was your love, but our encounter is no accident; hence, never did I go astray.
Embedded in my heart, is undying love for you.
I pondered not, for this is true love, and true love will not abandon its heart's pair.
So rather than mourn your love, I've fasted for your love.
Even as my heart hurts, I persevered in love, rather than collapse in love.
In an imperfect world, we lacked abilities to adhere to affectionate love, but I'll hold on.
Challenges want to take hold, but escorted are my thoughts and beliefs to your heart.
And tailored is my heart to love you eternally.
Even as I'm faced with the void, embraced, was moments vividly memorable.
Two people with preferences and differences, be you, spare from wrath.
In this imperfect world, our lights cannot be, dimmed, for our love has been preordained.
Amidst your absence, my heart grew to love you instead of retire from loving you.

Even in trying times of crumbling and failing love, I thirst for your love and your touch.
My heart lingers, harboured, and compiled love for you.
None of your wrongs can substantiate my departure from your love.
I angered not, for comprehension of the term love, appears boldly, even as we were apart.
Refrained from worries, sustain thoughts of encouragement, I forget how to fret
My heart has faced many interrogations, yet I've navigated and escalated in our love.
Afflicted, yet I've surrendered in love and escalated in stubbornness toward failure.
Engaging my heart and mind with thoughts of you, through challenges and sacrifices,
Comb my heart; you'll find vast possession of my love, disseminating for you.
A heart of perseverance, escalating in unquestionable, undying love for you.
The source of my love drive, here we are together, and all feels justified.
Devine strategy has allowed our love survival.
Our hearts collided in the vicinity of eternity, a precision, appointed for eternity.

Work in progress, a love once delayed but never denied.
Unpleasant acts are suffocated, dimmed, was the light of perfection.
We've faced challenges as we've embarked upon our destiny.
Accurate is the vicinity of our meeting; perseverance has ignored my heart injuries.
We've innocently faced trials, yet prevailed because of our passion and endurance.
Uninterrupted focus and discipline have brought me to you, minds navigating in one destination.
My love for you is not a dramatization but authenticated through faith.
Despite interrogations, uninterrupted and perpetuated is my love for you.
My mind radiates nothing but love for you, affliction fails, and love forever reigns.
Years of confessions are true, for my love undoubtedly belongs to you.
I love you this much hence why I did not quit.
Though Afflictions, with adjoining hands, in love, we still reign.
A love appointed, is a love, eternally treasure, for where love hails, interruptions fail.

Let's forever sail in love, for this love is designed for eternal success.
None will never understand, that which I've comprehended.
Now it's you and I together, until the end.

MOTHER

The road to comfort was long, But patient and strength, you're strong.
Months you've carried, and years you've raised
From loving you, I can't be distracted, my love for you will never be subtracted
For all you've been through, There can be no limit to the love I have for you
Undying love seems not to be enough; I wish I can fill every wanting and needing gap
My love will take the spot for you've thought me, how to appreciate and be compassionate
I will give you all things accessible to man for knowing your love eradicates my fear
You've got my love, and this is grand, Worth more than anything precious on this land
Your love dissolves my tears, for Your love is the strongest of anything, Your love is an everlasting filling.
many days I've seen you kneeled and revealed, With heart like steel
Yes I've seen you glazed and stared, The teardrops flowing from your eyes in fear
I've seen your weary heart in despair

Your heart has been to places for the upbringing of me, So let me set your heart free
Daily you've worried, where to find rice, You've worn a smile, but your heart has been in disguise
Putting food in the pot, you've exhausted your ways But look at me now, every bit of the struggle pays, so Enjoy your glory days
Yes I understand the discomfort and pain, But you will never have to face that life again
Though distasteful was the days, in me you still found joy
You prevented me from dust, Enjoy the divergent of Your supplication of love for the rope cant burst
This is your time, be uplifted, None cant put you down now that you have been lifted
you've Embrace me with love, Fought against disobedience and Broke chains of less to access more
The pathway to my door of more, You fought for the very best though vast was the trouble I brought
Mother, you're my everything, None will never understand your worth, the love you have within
For your love is empowering, it's your love that has shielded me from danger and sin
Your love surpasses all level of royalty; No price cant summarized the cost of your love

Your love enables me to proceed; you're the reason I can breed happily and free, at life fullest degree

I love you in all atmosphere, Thanks for showing me you care for your love makes me know love

My back was against the wall, and you never allow me to fall, you're always the one answering my call

Your love has placed me into a decent path; your love will always conquer my heart

I will stay pure and whole to you, for without you, how to love? I'd never have a clue

Your love has kept me out of the cell, and your love has saved me from hell

My moon and my sun, loving you, is the reason life is fun.

MY EVERYTHING

My little bee I knew you were the one for me, you came into my life and showed me all that I can be
You've opened up doors for me to explore my fantasies, you've taken me to a place call ecstasy.
You enable me to be loving, caring, and free; this is destiny, my morning coffee, and my midnight tea.
What the future holds Is something yet to be told, with you I've found a diamond, yes I've surpassed gold.
With you in my life, no price can summarize, I really love the way you entice.
Daily I embark on beautiful surprises; this has got to be real love, no catch, or disguises.
You supply love to my body, love to my life, everyone wants to learn from our enterprise.
Whenever I open my mouth, it's of you that I speak, baby, our love is on the fleet.
This love of ours is established on solid ground. No scale can't weigh it, not by the kilos or pound.
Indeed we are fulfilling a love surpass all royalty, work put in by you and me.
A love none will never know, you're the reason I can glow, for our love is truly Devine.
I disclosed to the world, and I'm so proud you're mine.

No other love is like ours, we worry not for this love is shielded by wings of a dove
No other love could be like this; you've swept me off my feet with just one kiss.
Aroma of sweet pitch pine, from all other activities I've resigned
Your love brings me plus signs; for you, I've been designed, this love has approached me at the right time.
And I'll always love you even in drought and famine, of all of life's love, you are my only lifeline.

THANK YOU

I wish I could give you all things accessible to man
Of your love, I can testify
But you've got my love, and this is grand
Worth more than any diamond own by man
Stronger than any building, you're so is filling
Mother's day is every day, the things you've done for me, I can't repay
Worry not for my love will never grow old or decay
For I love you mother, night and day
I will never be distracted from loving you, and your love will never be subtracted
No limit to the love I have for you
Yet it's nothing compared to things you've been through
You and Your faith has caused me to appreciate and be compassionate
I look at you with one glance, and I've come up with better plans
Can't you see, you're the reason I can be, you took my hands and taught me how to understand
I'm loved and free to my fullest degree
Thinking of you in all atmosphere
Only if you did not love me, where would I be

If you did not care, how the world would have viewed me
Thank you, mother, for you make me feel free

PROTECTING YOU

No thief, murderer, know your friend
I'm trying to guide you because I don't want your life to end
I'm your mother, and if you low me, I can be your best friend
I feel your pain, but the wrong company will induce prison term and great strain
From bad company, please refrain
Let my teaching be your domain for I feel your pain time again
I love you in days when you're weak and sick
Love you more than anyone of your chick
Love you way more than them telling you to come quick
To see you fall prey to crime would only make me sick
In my kitchen you freely cut the cheese slice thick
In the playground, I give you Popsicle by the many sticks
I'm always there when you're down and feeling sick

MISS YOU

I miss you, and that's a fact
I miss you, your presence I lack
I miss you baby, and I can't bring you back
I miss you, and it's no act
I miss you, he giveth and taketh back.

OVERCAME

You've submitted your love before me
Because of your love, I'm aiming for the sky
When I think of your love I cry for your love is so evident, I can't deny
My life starts with you and your love, my first teacher and everything
You'll never understand how your love erupts my feelings
Many never thought you'd be this uplifted
But none can't put down what God has gifted
To put food in the pot, you've exhausted your ways
But look at me now, the struggle pays
Enjoy your glory days and say goodbye to struggling days
Now tears of joy pours down your face
The road to comfort was long, but you held on, patience and strength, mother you're strong
Yes I know the discomfort, struggle and pain but for it all, you certainly deserve your gain
Though severe were the days, we still found joy, and though the struggle bold you still bought toys
They do not know your struggle nor your pain
Now they sit waiting for you to fall off your cliff

But conquer them father, destroy them wish
Where were they when we eat rice without fish?
Though the struggle you did not return me to dust
Enjoy what many lusts, for I love you, and this rope they can't bust.
For this love is just.

LAY YOU DOWN

I want to lay you on the ground
I want to emotionally, suck on your tongue
Graze on your body
Then whisper in your ears, baby undress me for I'm down
I want to rub your back then lead my hands to your pants
Only if you'd allow me with this chance
I'm going to take my time; you would get upset
Because you'll want to explode and I won't be there yet
Hand in hand, there we lay
Naked as we were born, night has turned into day
Then you turned and looked at me
Can we do this again? Don't say no
Because I'm down this time, can we not take it slow?
For I was starving, I immediately exploded.
Next time, can we get to the motive?
Because your way is like taking advantage.
Waiting for your love is like explosive.
Give me love if you've got love to give
Let lasting long be your motive

ITS YOU

It's no disgrace to access your warm embrace
One hug with you and the light shines in my face
I've searched my heart and all of my past you have to replace
What was love about I hadn't a clue
But ask me now, and I'll gladly say it's you

YOU AND YOUR LOVE

My heart can never be whole again
If from you and your love I must refrain
I know I did you wrong, but please return
For if you don't my heart will continue to burn
It will be this way for as long as you're gone
My friends told me to be strong
But I've tried and failed, for I've not got you to hold on.

DISTANCE

You've picked me up from where I fell
But then you've dropped me amid hell
A chance, I've pulled up my pants, for with you I want to dance eternally
Cancel keeping your distance
You seemed to have made me your enemy, but in your heart is where I want to be
For only your love knows my capabilities and without your love, death will take over me

THE ONE

We fought and nasty things we've said
Misunderstanding got to your head
She was lying on my bed, you showed up and quickly fled
She's the wife of Uncle Ted
For a maintenance of your love I beg
I still wish to be the one you wed
Can't you see, it was I who got on my knees
To you I plea, come back please
From my cheating ways, I have long ceased
Deeper and wider might be the sea
But there is only one girl for me
And with you I'll be

RETURN

I'm at the fountain thirsty as hell
But my heart won't allow me to drink for I'm not well
I tend to have it together, I've lost my feathers
No shielding my pride, for your return I cried
For many are the years I've hide
Believing someday it will all be great, and so I sit and wait
Then my love you've escaped, gone somewhere on a one-way slate
I can't eat the food in my plate, I've lost the ability to have faith
Like a lost woman I stand, not knowing my right hand from my left hand
I'm cold; you refused to make me warm
Only your hands protect me from harm
Turn me back with all your charm.

DON'T

Don't take me out of the light, only to leave me in the dark
Don't love me to part, don't love me to break my heart
Don't take me away from what I like, to leave me in fright
Don't take me it won't be right, if you'll want me just for a few nights
Don't take me to the top to drop me at the bottom, why they do that, I never fathom
Don't bring me to the top; I'm afraid of height
Don't take away my day for lonely nights
Don't take me heavy to drop me light
Don't take me; I'd rather stay here tonight
Don't take me if it's not for life
Don't take me if I won't be your wife

MY ONLY LOVE

Not talking too much
But when I want to be touched
I know where to go for such
Speaking English and Not Dutch
Only one person hands affects my crouch
I reside in his heart and secret path
From the day our love start
No other can glue me up nor stew me up
My forever has begun
And from those things we are done
For we look to each other for all pleasurable fun
In each other we find our moon and our sun
Never to make you sad or blue
I vow to love you faithfully true
Only you knows my weak spot
You alone brings out the silly in me
You apart taught me to love and feel free
For you've gotten on one knee
And proposed your love for me
I love the love you give
For your love encourages my heart to live.

YOU

The road ahead might be rocky
But I'll travel the path as long as you're with me
You completed my heart
My love, you've toiled
Embedded into your soul
Our bodies now drips with oil
My heart adores you from the day you came
I'll love you always until of love I'm drained
From the day you became mine
This is the beginning of a trip of our lifetime
Shielding each other with invisible feathers
We're a team
We full fill each other's dream
And that's the vanilla filled with cream
If you know what I mean
Your radiance and my sheen
We stand out like a durable machine
Here to stay
Not going no way kind of love
The very kind I've been dreaming of!
You alone make me feel at home
I will always want to be in your zone
A love so strong it Pearce through diamond

I knew you're the one the day you held my hand.

ME

On the level of me
It's all I can be
A simple one, with a desire to be free
And this is what I wish the world would see
And stop placing me into their category

WAIT

I looked at the fan; I watched it spin
Only if he could feel the love, I have within
Like that fan, I turn without a pause
If he'd love me back, he will give me rounds of applause
He says he's searching, but I am not wearing a mask
And loving him is my only task
To love me back, it's all I ask
The net I cast, I'm waiting, though I'm overtasked
I'll wait because you'll be my last
I'll patiently wait, I won't be fast
For this, your love will be the love, ill class
For the beauty of our love will be amass
And this love will be the blast that last

JUDGE NOT MY LOOKS

The content of my book is better than the cover
Give me that chance; you'll see I am a lover
Should you be sick, I will aide, ill fend until you' recover
I've got love to give in my unique flavour
Black, I maybe, but I am not a burnt-out tire, I've got a waist, you'll belief its rubber
When I'm done, you'll beg me to come over

HE

He says I've got exotic eyes and beautiful thighs, yet he tells me nothing but lies
He says he love the nappy in my hair and my sexy underwear
When he tells me things so delicious, it causes me to be suspicious
Every time he tells me things that are a plus, He's been unfairly ridiculous
But I know he's returning from his extra affairs, could he be a man who cares
He says his love for me he's enveloped, but ask me, and I'll say this love is like a slope
One time good and at times bad
At times upset and at times, glad
At times I wish he's the love I had
But at times, he makes my jealous
To keep this man I must, or maybe I'm afraid of new dust
The wrongs he dismisses with a hug and a kiss
Every time we argue about the miss
At times I pretend I don't see and just let him be,
At times it's like I'm in love with a stranger who has placed me in danger

But to this I have not wager
At times I know where he has been
So when he comes home, I pretend to be reading the magazine
A girl so slim and a girl so trim any man's heart I can easily win
So why is he doing this, it's a question I ask from within

ABOUT THE AUTHOR

Rhonda .A. Clarke is a Toronto-based poet who is a manager at Hammer Security; she has been writing poems from the tender age of nine. She is a music and fitness lover and loves dancing and understanding the cultures of the people she meets. She is outgoing and friendly and firmly believes that the smallest words tend to be the longest poem, and due to that fact, she always manages to carry a pen and paper to create poetry, whenever a thought comes to her mind. Rhonda is available for contact via Facebook and her youtube - Racs poeticalvibes / racspoeticalvibes@outlook.com

It's always a pleasure
knowing you.
I do hope you'll
enjoy this book

Thanks